# What Is Persuasive Writing?

Charlotte Guillain

heinemann
raintree

© 2016 Heinemann-Raintree
an imprint of Capstone Global Library, LLC
Chicago, Illinois

To contact Capstone Global Library please call 800-747-4992, or visit our web site
www.capstonepub.com

Edited by Clare Lewis and Penny West
Designed by Philippa Jenkins and Tim Bond
Picture research by Gina Kammer
Originated by Capstone Global Library Ltd
Produced by Helen McCreath
Printed and bound by CTPS

19  18  17  16  15
10 9 8 7 6 5 4 3 2 1

**Library of Congress Cataloging-in-Publication Data**
Guillain, Charlotte.
  What is persuasive writing? / Charlotte Guillain.
     pages cm—(Connect with text)
  Includes bibliographical references and index.
   ISBN 978-1-4109-8036-6 (hb)—ISBN 978-1-4109-8043-4 (ebook)  1. Persuasion (Rhetoric)—Juvenile
literature.  I. Title.
  P301.5.P47G85 2015
   808.02—dc23                    2015000245

**Acknowledgments**
The author and publisher are grateful to the following for permission to reproduce copyright material:
Alamy: © Graham Franks, 5; Capstone Studio: Karon Dubke, 13, 18, 20, 21, 22, 23, 24, 27, 28; Dreamstime:
© Elena Elisseeva, 7, © Konstantin Anisko, 29, © Serrnovik, 11, © Yvon52, 6; iStockphoto: mediaphotos,
9, 25; Shutterstock: Kinga, 4, Lisa F. Young, 26, MarclSchauer, 14, Milena Moiola, 15, Monkey Business
Images, 10, Radu Bercan, 8

# Contents

Some words are shown in bold, **like this**. You can find out what they mean by looking in the glossary.

# A World of Nonfiction

People read two different types of text: **fiction** and **nonfiction**. Writers create fiction when they write stories from their imagination. Nonfiction, on the other hand, is based on real facts. It gives readers information to help them learn and discover new ideas, places, and skills.

You are surrounded by nonfiction texts as you move around a city.

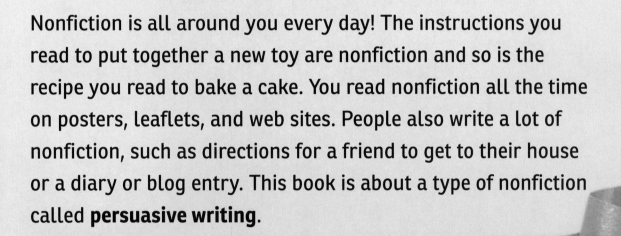

Information books are nonfiction texts that help us to learn about many different subjects.

Nonfiction is all around you every day! The instructions you read to put together a new toy are nonfiction and so is the recipe you read to bake a cake. You read nonfiction all the time on posters, leaflets, and web sites. People also write a lot of nonfiction, such as directions for a friend to get to their house or a diary or blog entry. This book is about a type of nonfiction called **persuasive writing**.

## Text around you

Think about all the nonfiction you have already read today. Have you read the text on any food packaging? Have you seen any posters or advertisements in magazines? If you've been on the Internet, you've probably read nonfiction text on web sites or instructions for games.

# What Is Persuasive Writing?

**Persuasive writing** is text that tries to persuade its reader to agree with a certain point of view. The writer presents one side of an argument and gives the reader reasons to make him or her agree.

You might write persuasive texts in school. You will also see them wherever you go. A review of a movie in a newspaper or on a web site is persuasive writing. The writer is giving you an **opinion** of the movie and presents examples to get you to agree. A writer of advertisements is trying to persuade you to buy or do something. If a charity gives you a leaflet asking for money, it will include persuasive writing to convince you to give money to the cause.

Many groups produce posters and leaflets to persuade the public to support them.

# Text in history

You can find information leaflets on lots of different topics. They often try to persuade us to agree with one opinion. During World War II (1939–1945), both sides sent leaflets to enemy soldiers trying to persuade them to stop fighting. This leaflet from the German government tried to persuade American, British, and Canadian soldiers to stop fighting by promising safety and comfort in Germany.

## The German People Offers Peace.

The new German democratic government has this programme:

### "The will of the people is the highest law."

The German people wants quickly to end the slaughter.

The new German popular government therefore has offered an

### Armistice

and has declared itself ready for

### Peace

on the basis of justice and reconciliation of nations.

It is the will of the German people that it should live in peace with all peoples, honestly and loyally.

What has the new German popular government done so far to put into practice the will of the people and to prove its good and upright intentions?

a) **The new German government has appealed to President Wilson to bring about peace.**

**It has recognized and accepted all the principles which President Wilson proclaimed as a basis for a general lasting peace of justice among the nations.**

b) The new German government has solemnly declared its readiness to **evacuate** Belgium and to restore it.

c) The new German government is ready to come to an honest understanding with France about.

### Alsace-Lorraine.

d) The new German government has restricted the **U-boat War.**

### No passengers steamers not carrying troops or war material will be attacked in future.

e) The new German government has declared that it will **withdraw all** German troops back over the German frontier.

f) — The new German government has asked the Allied Governments to name commissioners to agree upon the practical measures of the evacuation of Belgium and France.

These are the deeds of the new German popular government. Can these be called mere words, or bluff, or propaganda?

Who is to blame, if an armistice is not called now?

Who is to blame if daily thousands of brave soldiers needlessly have to shed their blood and die?

Who is to blame, if the hitherto undestroyed towns and villages of France and Belgium sink in ashes?

Who is to blame, if hundreds of thousands of unhappy women and children are driven from their homes to hunger and freeze?

## The German people offers its hand for peace.

# What Are the Features of Persuasive Writing?

**Persuasive writing** often has the following features:

- A writer usually starts with several sentences that introduce the topic. Often the subject of persuasive writing is something that people have different **opinions** about.

- After introducing the subject, a writer then says what his or her opinion is. The writer uses examples to show why this opinion is right. A writer will include lots of details and facts to back up what he or she thinks.

The text on a persuasive poster needs to be very simple and clear, so people get the message!

## Text tips!

When you are writing a piece of persuasive text, always be clear what your opinions are. If you are unsure what you think, it will be much harder to persuade someone else to agree with a particular point of view.

- A writer of persuasive text often tries to make the reader feel a certain way. If the writer can affect the reader's emotions, this can really help to persuade the reader to agree with the writer's opinion.

- A piece of persuasive writing usually ends with a summary that repeats what the writer's opinion is. The reader should be in no doubt what the writer thinks.

# What Sort of Language Is Used in Persuasive Writing?

In most examples of **persuasive writing**, the writer uses the **present tense**. He or she is writing about what is happening now.

Many persuasive texts start out with a question. This makes the reader think about what his or her **opinion** is on the subject. If the reader doesn't already have an answer, the writer has arguments to persuade him or her to agree.

It may help to talk to someone about a subject before forming an opinion about it.

Persuasive text uses words that try to appeal to the reader's senses and emotions. Because of this, it can sometimes use language that is creative, like **fiction**. You may also notice lots of words such as "but," "so," "however," and "therefore." These kinds of words help to make the writer's argument more persuasive.

## Text around you

Find some examples of persuasive texts, such as book reviews, advertisements, or leaflets. How does the writing make you feel? See how many examples you can find of the words "but," "so," "however," and "therefore" and circle them. Can you use these words in the next piece of persuasive text you write?

# Using Pictures in Persuasive Writing

Like other types of **nonfiction** text, writers often include pictures and graphics alongside persuasive text. Essays or leaflets that try to persuade the reader to support a particular point of view often include graphs and charts. These images are a quick, visual way to give **evidence** to support the writer's arguments. There might also be striking photographs to appeal to the reader's feelings. For example, a wildlife charity might show shocking photographs of animals' homes being destroyed. This gets an emotional reaction from the reader.

## Text in history

Most posters we see today include photographs. Have you seen any that use artwork? Before photography was invented, many persuasive posters used amazing paintings and prints. Some of these posters were real works of art, and the pictures appealed to the public as much as the persuasive text.

This advertisement uses a photograph to support its message.

Advertisements often include interesting or unusual photographs to catch the reader's attention. Sometimes they show beautiful images to make the reader want to buy the product. Book reviews usually include a picture of the book cover. Movie reviews may include a still photograph that shows the main actors in the movie.

# Thinking About the Reader

When you are writing a piece of **nonfiction**, think about your reader. Do you know who the reader will be, or could it be anyone? Decide whether to use **formal** or **informal** language. If you don't know who will be reading your **persuasive writing**, and if you're writing about a serious topic, then it is usually best to write in a formal way. If you know who your reader will be, you know the person well, and your subject is fun, then it might be better to write informally.

If you're writing formal language, it's a good idea to use a dictionary or **thesaurus** to help you with unfamiliar words.

## Text tips!

If you're not sure whether you're reading a formal or informal piece of writing, try reading it out loud. If it sounds like you are talking with a friend, then the writing is informal. If there are words you wouldn't normally use when talking, then the writing is probably more formal.

What might your reader already think about the subject you are writing about? Might he or she already have an **opinion**, or might the topic be unfamiliar? If you are trying to change someone's mind, you'll need lots of **evidence** to persuade him or her. If you are introducing your reader to a new subject, you will need to take time to explain it clearly.

# A Book or Movie Review

Make sure you finish the book or movie before you form your **opinion** and write a review. If you don't know what happens at the end, your arguments might not be very persuasive!

Take some notes and think about your opinion. Did you like it or not? Why? You need to give reasons and examples to back up your opinions. If you didn't like the movie or book, can you think of something positive about it to give your review some balance? Compare the book or movie to other works to help the reader understand what it's like.

## Text around you

There are lots of web sites for kids that provide book reviews written by other kids. Visit one of these web sites (see page 31). How do the reviewers persuade you to read the books they have enjoyed?

It can be hard to decide which movies to see without reviews to help you choose.

Make sure you don't give away any important plot twists or the ending! If you enjoyed the book or movie, then you need to persuade your readers to go out and find it themselves!

# Advertisements

Advertisements are usually short pieces of text. They work very hard to persuade the reader to buy or do something. The writers of ads often use language and images in clever or surprising ways to make the reader pay attention or laugh.

Some ads include information or graphics that prove to the reader that a product is worth buying and why it's better than other products. For example, the ad might mention a survey that tells the reader that 9 out of 10 people prefer its product.

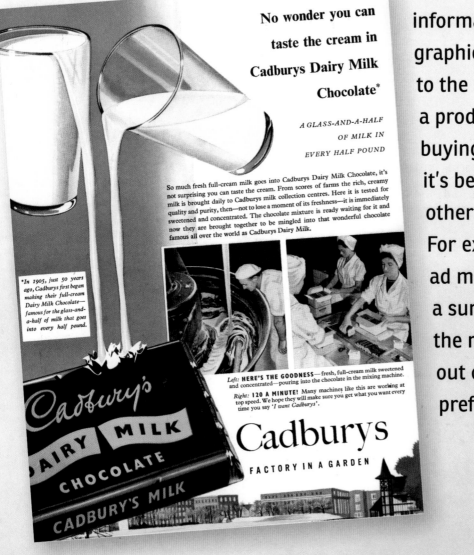

No wonder you can taste the cream in Cadburys Dairy Milk Chocolate*

*A GLASS-AND-A-HALF OF MILK IN EVERY HALF POUND*

So much fresh full-cream milk goes into Cadburys Dairy Milk Chocolate, it's not surprising you can taste the cream. From scores of farms the rich, creamy milk is brought daily to Cadburys milk collection centres. Here it is tested for quality and purity, then—not to lose a moment of its freshness—it is immediately sweetened and concentrated. The chocolate mixture is ready waiting for it and now they are brought together to be mingled into that wonderful chocolate famous all over the world as Cadburys Dairy Milk.

*In 1905, just 50 years ago, Cadburys first began making their full-cream Dairy Milk Chocolate— famous for the glass-and-a-half of milk that goes into every half pound.

*Left:* **HERE'S THE GOODNESS**—fresh, full-cream milk sweetened and concentrated—pouring into the chocolate in the mixing machine.

*Right:* **120 A MINUTE!** Many machines like this are working at top speed. We hope they will make sure you get what you want every time you say 'I want Cadburys'.

Cadbury's DAIRY MILK CHOCOLATE CADBURY'S MILK

## Cadburys
FACTORY IN A GARDEN

Ads in magazines and newspapers have to stand out so that they will catch the reader's eye.

Ads are usually written to make readers think their life will be better if they buy this product or do this activity. Sometimes the text in ads can be friendly and **informal**, especially if the ad is aimed at young people.

## Text around you

Can you think of an ad you have seen recently, either on television or as a poster? What do you think helped you to remember it? Was it the colors or the language used? Did it have a colorful or exciting photograph? Did it make you laugh? Lots of ads stay in our minds because they are funny!

# How to Write Persuasively: Creating an Advertisement

Write an advertisement to persuade your friend that he or she has to try your favorite snack!

1. Think about your favorite snack and jot down some words to describe it. What **adjectives** could you use to describe how eating it feels? Don't be afraid to go over the top!

2. Tell the reader what makes this snack better than other snacks. Is it tasty or especially healthy? Will it give the reader energy?

3. Think about how you can grab the reader's attention. Maybe you could ask him or her a question at the start of the ad or you could say something funny. Can you write a **slogan** for your ad? This should be a few words that use **rhyme** or **alliteration** to make a snappy, memorable statement about your snack.

4. Write or type your ad and check that your spelling and grammar are correct. The reader might not trust your ad if there are mistakes in your writing!

5. Add a photo of the snack or you eating it. Or you could print out your ad and draw a picture to go with the text.

6. Give your ad to someone to read. Does it make the person want to go and buy the snack?

# Leaflets

Lots of organizations produce leaflets and posters about their work. These leaflets give people information, but they also try to persuade readers to support the organization. This support might be volunteering, making a donation, or buying a product. For example, a charity might create a poster to catch people's attention and tell them why they need their help.

THE WAR ON HUNGER

SYRIA CRISIS AP
Two Years Too

Leaflets use large headings and graphics to make sure their message is noticed.

When a writer creates the text for a poster or leaflet, he or she needs to provide a lot of **evidence** to support the arguments. The text needs to show that the work the organization is doing is worthwhile. Leaflets might include case studies of specific examples of the organization's work, with quotations and photos of people involved. They often also include charts and diagrams to present accurate **data**.

## Text tips!

If you're writing a poster to persuade people to do something, try showing your readers how the situation affects them. This will help you to change their minds.

# How to Write Persuasively:
# Making a Poster

Write a poster to tell people about an event at your school. You need to persuade as many people as possible to come!

1. Plan your poster. What is the main information you need to include? You don't want to add too much text or people will miss important details. What images can you use?

2. Write the heading for your poster. It needs to be large and eye-catching and sum up what the event is about. People need to be able to read the heading from a distance— hopefully this will draw them in to come closer and read the details.

SCHOOL
FAIR
Date: Saturday, July 14
Time: 1:00 pm
Place: School Hall

3. Describe what will happen at the event. Use **adjectives** and **adverbs** to make it sound exciting. Make readers feel like they will be missing out if they don't come!

4. Include important information such as the date, time, and place of the event. Make sure these details stand out clearly.

5. Check that all the information, spelling, and grammar on your poster are correct.

6. Add drawings or photos to your poster. Try to make it as colorful and attractive as possible.

7. Put your poster up in a busy place where people can easily read it. Good luck with your event!

# Persuasive Essay

**Persuasive writing** is sometimes found in newspapers and magazines. People write persuasive articles to say what they think about a subject. It could be happening in the news or be something that affects the readers. These articles, or essays, are different from the reports in newspapers, because they don't have to give both sides of the argument.

## Briefing

### The fate of Britain's woodlands

*The Archbishop of Canterbury and a host of celebrities are calling on the Government to reverse its woodlands policy*

**What are they all so worried about?**
England's forests being put at risk. Back in October, shortly after its budget was cut by 29% in the spending review, the Department for Environment, Food and Rural Affairs (Defra) announced it was selling off about 15% of woods managed by the Forestry Commission in England to private developers and "civil society", hoping to raise £100m in the process. Then, in November, the Government started talking about a "very substantial disposal of public forest estate, which could go to the extent of it all". The big fear is that the proposed sell-off – potentially the biggest change in land ownership since the Second World War – will not only restrict access to woodland but lead to the ripping up of woods to build holiday villages and golf courses or to accommodate power suppliers.

*Sherwood Forest: will they cut it down?*

**How much of the country is covered in woodland?**
About 12%, more than at any time since the 1750s, according to the Forestry Commission, and not far off the 15% recorded in the Domesday Book in 1086. Britain is a naturally forested land (it still has woodland habitats – blends of ash, beech, hazel, oak and yew – dating from the Ice Age), but that forest cover was stripped back during the agricultural revolution. By the mid-18th century much of it was restored, only to be cut down again for ship-building during the Napoleonic wars, and then decimated for the furnaces and factories of the Industrial Revolution. By the time the Forestry Commission was set up in 1919 – to ensure there would be no shortage of pit props in any future war – a mere 4%

**And how much belongs to the state?**
Overall, 28% of UK woodlands are controlled by the Forestry Commission (strictly speaking, the environment secretary "owns" them), but the percentage varies widely across the realm. In Northern Ireland it owns 70%, while the Forestry Commission Scotland owns 36% (8.5% of Scotland's land area), and is a major producer of British Christmas trees. (With 1,640,000 acres, it's the biggest landlord in Scotland, surpassing the Duke of Buccleuch's 270,000 acres and the RSPB's 124,172.) But in England less than a third of woodland is publicly owned: 18% belongs to the Forestry Commission, including heritage woodlands like the Forest of Dean and the New Forest, and 6% to local authorities. Thanks in part to woodland's exemption from inheritance tax, the percentage of private owners has shot up in recent years to about half (most of them not so much farmers as rich urbanites using woods as an amenity); 14% is owned by private businesses; less than 1% by timber businesses.

**So why worry if more of it goes into private hands?**
There's no need to, say supporters of the new policy. Like many a nationalised industry, the Forestry Commission has a lousy record as a timber producer – it has almost always run at a loss – and its recent conversion to the role of environmental guardian has created an...
and as a re...
grant leases...
projects. Far...

When writers publish persuasive articles, readers often go online to say how they feel.

It's a good idea to discuss a topic with your friends first, to see what the different opinions are.

You might have to write a persuasive essay in school. This could be a piece of writing on a topic where you explain what your **opinion** is and provide examples and **evidence** to back it up. You need to think about what the arguments on the other side might be, too. Come up with reasons that show why the other side is wrong. It's important that your essay has a strong **conclusion** at the end.

## Text tips!

When you have written a persuasive essay, try reading it out loud. Sometimes hearing your words will tell you if you need to be more persuasive in your arguments.

# How to Write Persuasively: Writing an Essay

Plan your essay carefully and decide what your **opinion** is. Make a list of the main arguments you want to write about.

1. Look at your list. What **evidence** or examples do you have to show why your arguments are right?

2. Write your essay. Give it a clear **introduction** that says what your essay will be about and what your opinion is. Follow this with your main argument and evidence to back this up. Then add your other arguments.

3. Think about how you can affect the reader's feelings so that he or she is more likely to agree with you.

4. Try to use words such as "however," "therefore," "because," and "so."

5. Give your essay a strong **conclusion**. Suggest again that the reader should agree with you.

6. Check your spelling and grammar. The reader is more likely to be persuaded if he or she is not distracted by mistakes in your writing!

7. Type your essay and print it out. Now share it with someone and see if that person agrees with your opinion after finishing reading your essay!

# Glossary

**adjective** word that describes a noun

**adverb** word that describes a verb

**alliteration** when words start with the same letter

**conclusion** ending to a piece of writing

**data** pieces of information

**evidence** facts or quotes to prove what is being said

**fiction** story that has been made up

**formal** following the expected rules

**informal** relaxed and not following all the rules

**introduction** beginning of a piece of writing that explains what topic the writing will cover

**nonfiction** writing about real-life facts

**opinion** what someone thinks or believes

**persuasive writing** writing that tries to get the reader to agree with the writer

**present tense** writing that describes events and situations that are happening now

**rhyme** when words have the same sounds

**slogan** words used to sum up a message or advertise something

**thesaurus** book that suggests alternative words with a similar meaning

# Find Out More

To learn more about how to gather, organize, and present your ideas, you could read the following books. The web sites listed below might give you more guidelines for writing a persuasive text as well as examples of some good ones.

## Books

Nolan, Chris, and Lauren Spencer. *Writing to Persuade* (Write Like a Pro). New York: Rosen, 2012.

Pulver, Beth A., and Donald C. Adcock. *Organizing and Using Information* (Information Literacy Skills). Chicago: Heinemann Library, 2009.

Vickers, Rebecca. *Making Better Sentences: The Power of Structure and Meaning* (Find Your Way with Words). Chicago: Heinemann Library, 2013.

Vickers, Rebecca. *Types of Words: Unleashing Powerful Parts of Speech* (Find Your Way with Words). Chicago: Heinemann Library, 2013.

## Web sites

Facthound offers a safe, fun way to find Internet sites related to this book. All of the sites on Facthound have been researched by our staff.

Here's all you do:
Visit www.facthound.com
Type in this code: 9781410980366

# Index